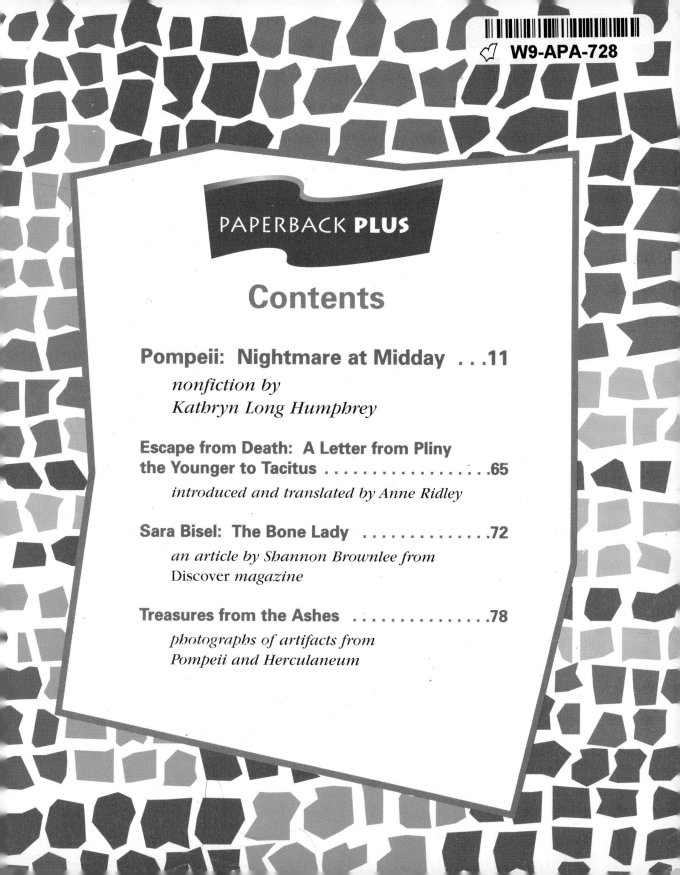

PAPERBACK **PLUS**

Contents

KATHRYN LONG HUMPHREY

While visiting London, England, in 1976, Kathryn Long Humphrey saw a fascinating exhibit on Pompeii. Some twelve years later, she began to write a book about this ancient city. Humphrey traveled to Italy to see the ruins and was disappointed at first. Pompeii was closed to visitors  because of a strike! Luckily, the site was reopened later in the week, and Humphrey got to experience the thrill of walking through the ruins of the ancient city. She even climbed Mount Vesuvius!

KATHRYN LONG HUMPHREY

POMPEII

NIGHTMARE AT MIDDAY

HOUGHTON MIFFLIN COMPANY

BOSTON

ATLANTA   DALLAS   GENEVA, ILLINOIS   PALO ALTO   PRINCETON

Acknowledgments

Grateful acknowledgment is made for use of the following material:

Text

1 *Pompeii: Nightmare at Midday*, by Kathryn Long Humphrey. Copyright © 1990 by Kathryn Long Humphrey. Reprinted by permission of Franklin Watts. **72** "Sara Bisel: The Bone Lady," by Shannon Brownlee, from *Discover* magazine. Copyright © 1984 by *Discover* magazine. Reprinted by permission.

Illustrations

66 Chris Costello.

Photography

2 Courtesy of Kathryn Humphrey; David Hiser/Photographers/Aspen (cover). **13** Scala/Art Resource, NY. **14** Giraudon/Art Resource, NY. **16** Scala/Art Resource, NY. **19** The Bettmann Archive. **21** David Mlotok. **28** John Verde/Photo Researchers. **36** Marvullo/Photomontage. **38** John Verde/Photo Researchers (t); Marvullo/Photomontage (b). **40** David Hiser/Photographers/Aspen. **43** David Mlotok. **48** David Mlotok. **51** Scala/Art Resource, NY. **55** Scala/Art Resource, NY. **56** Photo Researchers. **59** David Mlotok (t); John Verde/Photo Researchers (b). **60** Marvullo/Photomontage. **65** Giraudon/Art Resource, NY. **65–71** Tony Scarpetta (background). **67** The Art Museum, Princeton University. Museum purchase, gift of Franklin H. Kissner. **68–69** Illustration by Ken Marschall from *The Secrets of Vesuvius,* a Scholastic/Madison Press book. Design and compilation © 1990 The Madison Press Limited, text © 1990 Sara C. Bisel and family and The Madison Press Limited. **70** Homer Sykes/Woodfin Camp & Associates. **71** Ancient Art and Architecture Collection. **72** © Joe McNally. All rights reserved. **72–73** Vittoriano Rastelli. **74** Lloyd Townsend/© 1984 *Discover* magazine. **75** Vittoriano Rastelli (t); Massimo Cappon/Mondadori Press (b). **76** © Joe McNally. All rights reserved. **77** © Joe McNally. All rights reserved (t); Royal Ontario Museum, Toronto, Canada (b). **78** O. Louis Mazzatenta, © National Geographic Society (t); Museo Archeologico Nazionale, Naples, Italy (m); Art Resource, NY (b). **78–79** CM Dixon. **79** Ancient Art and Architecture Collection (tl); Robert Frerck/Woodfin Camp & Associates (tr); CM Dixon (br). **80** Museo Archeologico Nazionale, Naples, Italy. Photo by Erich Lessing/Art Resource, NY (tl); Museo Archeologico Nazionale, Naples, Italy (tr, m, bl); Ancient Art and Architecture Collection (br).

Houghton Mifflin Edition, 1996
Copyright © 1996 by Houghton Mifflin Company. All rights reserved.

Printed in the U.S.A.

ISBN 0-395-73265-4

23456789-B-98 97 96 95

For
my husband, Dick,
with love

Quotes on pages 20, 24, 25, and 34 are from *The Letters of the Younger Pliny*, translated by Betty Radice, and published by Viking-Penguin, New York, © 1963, 1969.

Cover photograph courtesy of
Photographers/Aspen (David Hiser)

Map and diagram by Joe LeMonnier

Photographs courtesy of: Art Resource: pp. 13, 16, 51, 55, (Scala), 14 (Giraudon); The Bettmann Archive: p. 19; David Mlotok: pp. 21, 43, 48, 59 top; Photo Researchers: pp. 28, 38 top, 59 bottom, (all John Verde), 56; Marvullo: pp. 36, 38 bottom, 60; Photographers/Aspen: p. 40 (David Hiser).

CONTENTS

POMPEII

I

THE MOUNTAIN EXPLODES

Around noon on August 24, A.D. 79, the top of Mt. Vesuvius blew off. Burning stones, red-hot pumice, and ash blasted out of the volcano and shot 12 miles (19 km) into the air. People in Pompeii, Italy, heard a deafening roar. They screamed in fear.

The tall slender cloud of ash and rock spread out like an umbrella. The bright midday sky turned dark.

Small earth tremors had shaken Pompeii for several days before the volcano erupted. The sea boiled from the heat under the earth, like a pan of water boils from the heat of a burner. Streams dried up. Even the animals knew something was wrong.

The cows made strange noises. Dogs, cats, and rats escaped from the city.

August 24 had started as a normal day in Pompeii. A dog chained inside a house barked at people passing by. Children played with dolls and stick horses and used nuts and small stones as marbles. Some boys pretended to be gladiators fighting wild animals. Others dressed in armor like soldiers. Some played with small carts pulled by birds or goats.

At one house, slaves roasted a pig in the oven. A slave at another house fixed a lady's hair in the latest style.

A shopkeeper sold hot and cold drinks. A baker named Modestus put eighty-one loaves of bread in his oven. Gladiators relaxed in the wine shop. Priests ate their lunch of eggs and fish.

People gathered at Pompeii's Forum, or town center, and talked about the coming election. They read the news written on the walls the way people today read newspapers. Some bought fruit at the Forum market.

Then suddenly Vesuvius blew up, and the people ran from the Forum in every direction. The gladiators fled from the wine shop. The priests left their eggs and fish. The shopkeeper dropped money from the latest sale on the counter and hurried away. The baker darted off with flour still on his clothes.

*Over forty bakeries have been discovered
in Pompeii. Modestus's shop had four
mills and an adjacent oven.*

As Vesuvius erupted, the course of history forever changed: within hours, Pompeii and Herculaneum would disappear.

The lady forgot about having her hair styled and ran. The slaves left the pig roasting in the oven. The children stopped playing and screamed for their parents. And the dog twisted and pulled on his chain, but could not break loose.

About thirty minutes after the volcano erupted, a shower of hot ash poured down on the city. Pea-sized pieces of pumice, a lightweight rock filled with tiny holes, fell on everything and everyone.

A few people were hit by larger rocks torn from the volcano. Many tied pillows on their heads for protection against the hot ash and rocks. They shielded their faces with their hands or sleeves. The burning ash and rocks fell everywhere. The people of Pompeii seemed to be suffering through a nightmare—but they were wide awake.

Families stumbled along in darkness on the pumice-covered slabs of pavement toward the gates of the city. Parents and slaves carried small children. Many of Pompeii's twenty thousand people ran for their lives. They stampeded like animals. Some pushed their way through the sea gate hoping to escape by boat. Some freed horses or mules from carts and rode away on them.

Birds were killed in flight and dropped from the sky. Fish died at sea and washed on shore.

The wind blew ash and pumice all over the

*Although many walls still stand, most
roofs were torn off by lava or collapsed
under the weight of the ash.*

city—every hour six more inches piled up! By late afternoon a two-foot blanket of ash covered everything in Pompeii.

Roofs caved in from the weight of the ash and killed people under them. Bridges broke. Giant waves crashed against the shore. Ash fell into the harbor. It mixed with the water and turned to mush.

People who didn't leave right away had trouble opening their doors. Some chopped holes through the walls of their houses to escape.

Not everyone was able to leave Pompeii. Some people were too old or too sick. Others thought it would be safer to stay inside their houses. Some wasted precious minutes gathering up money and jewelry.

Those who waited too long never escaped.

II

EYEWITNESS ACCOUNT

A navy admiral named Pliny the Elder watched the strange cloud from the Roman naval base at Cape Misenum, across the Bay of Naples from Vesuvius. Sometimes the cloud was white. Sometimes it was gray from the ash.

Pliny the Elder was an expert in science and wrote a book called *Natural History*. He wanted to go closer to study the cloud and ordered a boat to take him across the bay. Before he left he heard that a friend was stranded at a beach town near Vesuvius. He ordered a warship to try to rescue as many people as possible.

His teenage nephew, Pliny the Younger, stayed behind in Misenum. After the eruption was over,

Pliny the Younger recorded his observation
of the erupting Vesuvius.

Pliny the Younger heard about his uncle's rescue mission. He later wrote a letter to Tacitus, a historian who wanted to know what happened. This letter was published and can still be read today.

He wrote that Pliny the Elder "headed straight for the place of danger. He was entirely fearless. Ashes were already falling, hotter and thicker as the ship drew near."

The helmsman advised Pliny the Elder to turn back, but he kept going. Ash and floating pumice blocked the harbor where he planned to dock. He changed course and went ashore at the town of Stabiae, four miles south of Pompeii.

Fires blazed on the mountain. Pliny the Elder tried to make his friends feel less afraid. He told them the fires were only bonfires left by country people. Pliny and his friends went into a house. He lay down and took a nap to try to convince them there was nothing to worry about.

During the night, ash and pumice piled up outside the door of the room where Pliny slept. His friends woke him. They were afraid he might not be able to get out of the room if he stayed much longer.

The group argued about whether to stay inside or go out. Inside, the rooms trembled "with violent shocks." Outside, burning rocks fell.

This photo shows what the trembling
earth and running lava did to
the floors of ancient rooms.

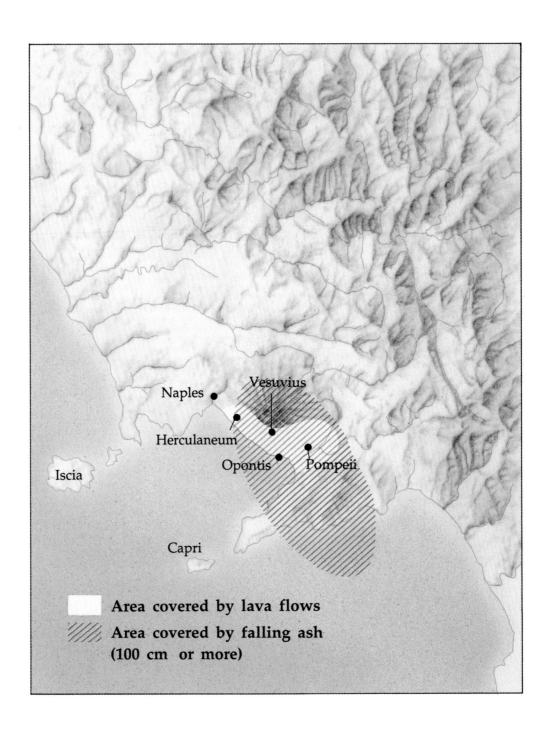

Area covered by lava flows

Area covered by falling ash (100 cm or more)

Naples

Vesuvius

Herculaneum

Opontis

Pompeii

Iscia

Capri

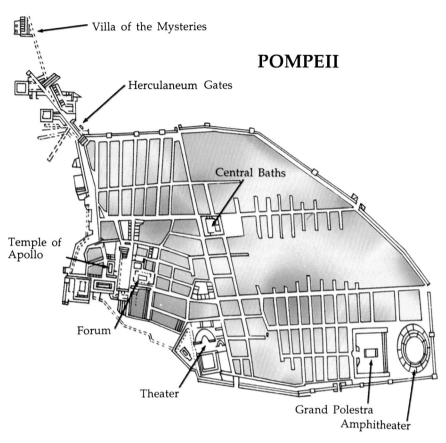

Villa of the Mysteries

POMPEII

Herculaneum Gates

Central Baths

Temple of
Apollo

Forum

Theater

Grand Polestra

Amphitheater

ITALY

Area of
Detail

Naples

Sicily

They decided they would be safer outdoors. They tied pillows over their heads, took their lamps, and went out. Even though it was now morning, the ash made it so dark outside that it was "blacker . . . than any ordinary night."

Pliny the Elder wanted to take the people to safety in his warship, but the waves were too wild.

Ash from the volcano clogged his lungs, which were already weak. His friends spread a sheet on the ground for him to lie on. As he rested, he kept asking for cold water to drink.

Suddenly, there was a giant cloud of fire. People smelled sulfur and ran. Two slaves stayed behind and helped Pliny stand up. But he choked on the fumes and fell down dead. Some people who escaped from Stabiae told Pliny the Younger what happened.

Even in Misenum, Pliny the Younger felt the shocks from the volcano. He later described his own experiences in a second letter to the historian. "That night the shocks were so violent that everything felt as if it were not only shaken but overturned."

In the morning, the buildings rocked back and forth. Pliny the Younger and his mother left Misenum with many others from the town. Carts on the road slid in every direction. People put heavy stones in them to weigh them down, but the carts kept sliding.

In the cloud above Vesuvius, fire exploded like giant flashes of lightning. "The cloud sank and covered the sea . . . Ashes were falling, and a thick black cloud came up behind spreading over the earth like a flood. . . . Then darkness fell . . . as if a lamp had been put out in a closed room."

Grown-ups and children screamed and shouted. "Some were calling to their parents, others to their children or to their wives, trying to recognize them by their voices. Some prayed for death. . . ."

"Some thought the universe had fallen into darkness forever."

III

NO PLACE TO HIDE

After Vesuvius erupted, the cloud of gas, ash, and stone shot into the air for about eighteen hours. Sometimes it rose as high as twelve miles (19 km). The ash fell on people as far away as Africa. Then the volcano's energy weakened for a while.

The long narrow cloud wobbled like the water from a hose when the pressure is turned down. About midnight a river of hot ash, rocks, and gas poured down the side of Vesuvius at 60 miles (96 km) an hour. This was called an avalanche. This avalanche did not come near Pompeii, but it buried Herculaneum, a city on the other side of Vesuvius.

Pressure from the volcano became stronger again, and the gases and ash shot into the air again. The cloud rose and fell. By six o'clock the next morning, three avalanches of hot ash, rocks, and gas had rushed down the mountain. Even though one hit the north wall of Pompeii, none went inside the walls. But ash and pumice had been falling on the city all night. Nine feet (2.7 m) of it was piled on top of everything.

Then, at 6:30 A.M. on August 25, another river of superheated gases, rocks and ash crashed down the mountain. This time the avalanche went inside the walls of Pompeii. It tore off many roofs and knocked down everything higher than the 9 feet (2.7 m) of ash. The heat, ash, and gases clogged people's lungs and choked them to death. Gases even seeped inside the buildings.

Volcano expert Dr. Haraldur Sigurdsson has written that at about the same time this avalanche reached Pompeii, tons of very fine ash fell. The ash immediately buried everyone in the position they were in when they died.

The fumes killed people inside their houses as well as outside. People held each other for comfort and were frozen with their arms around each other.

*People were killed quickly at Pompeii. Many
were found frozen in living positions.*

A woman died clutching her jewels. A slave died draped over plates he had dropped. A man begging outside the city gate died with his sack.

At least 2,000 people were killed and buried by the ashes covering Pompeii.

And the ash continued to fall.

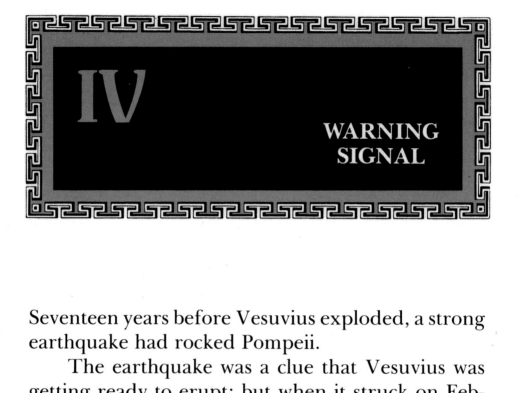

IV
WARNING SIGNAL

Seventeen years before Vesuvius exploded, a strong earthquake had rocked Pompeii.

The earthquake was a clue that Vesuvius was getting ready to erupt; but when it struck on February 5 in A.D. 62, people did not understand the warning. Vesuvius seemed to be a peaceful mountain; hardly anyone thought it was a volcano.

The earthquake was probably caused by pressure under the volcano. A volcano is a hole in the earth's crust that lets gases from inside the earth escape. Scientists think that about 40 miles (64 km) below the ground, heat melts the rock. When it does, gases are produced, and these gases in the melted rock try to escape. They push the hot melted rock, called "magma," toward the surface of the earth.

As the magma moves up, it often forms a pipe to the surface. Pressure pushes the magma out through a hole in the ground. Once the melted rock gets outside the earth, it is called lava.

Sometimes the melted rock hardens in the pipe as it bubbles up. This hard rock blocks the opening and the gas cannot escape. The longer it has been since a volcano has erupted, the more blocked the hole is and the more pressure there is from trapped gas.

In the first century A.D. Vesuvius had not erupted for about 1,200 years. The pipe was so blocked, it needed a strong blast to clear it.

Scientists now think Vesuvius was trying to erupt when the earthquake took place in A.D. 62, but the hole was too clogged. A giant explosion was needed to break through the hardened rock.

When Vesuvius finally erupted, there was no runny lava. The magma was thick and full of bubbles from gas. When the foamy magma was pushed into the air, it cooled so fast that the foam froze into the rock we call pumice. Pumice is like a sponge made of rock. It is so full of tiny holes it is light enough to float on water.

The blast that finally opened the pipe was as strong as a nuclear bomb. Gases shot into the air and held up the enormous cloud of ash and rock. This

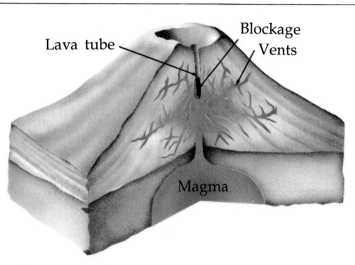

Lava tube

Blockage

Vents

Magma

The top diagram shows a volcano with a blocked pipeline. When the pressure from the gases in the magma becomes strong enough it forces the blockage out of the way and the volcano erupts. The bottom diagram shows a Plinian-type explosion.

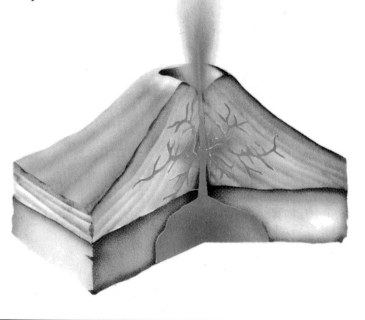

eruption of Vesuvius in A.D. 79 was ten times as powerful as that of Mount Saint Helens in 1980.

Today, the kind of volcano that explodes is called a Plinian eruption. It is named after Pliny the Younger, the teenager who watched Vesuvius erupt from across the Bay of Naples.

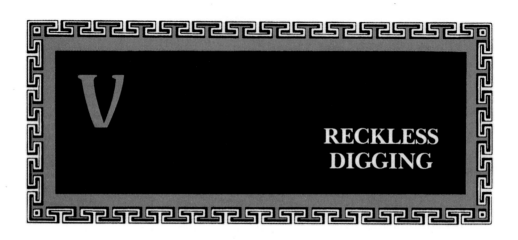

V

RECKLESS DIGGING

After Vesuvius erupted, gladiators, bakers, wine makers, and others who escaped from Pompeii were homeless. Their only clothes were the ones they wore out of the city.

Wives had lost their husbands. Children had lost their parents and were orphans. "Pompeii was buried deep in ashes like snow drifts," Pliny wrote. At first the days were still dark, because ash filled the air. Little by little, the sky became lighter.

Earthquakes continued for several more days, but finally they, too, stopped. People went back to look at the hill of ash that covered Pompeii. Some of them made tunnels and dug out their furniture and jewelry. Others sent slaves to dig. A few rooftops stuck out and guided people to their homes.

People burrowed tunnels and scribbled on the walls. One person, probably a Christian or Jew, wrote "Sodom and Gomorrah" on a wall. Sodom and Gomorrah were wicked cities mentioned in the Bible. They were both destroyed by fire.

It was dangerous to dig in Pompeii. Poison gas was trapped under the ash. Finally, people stopped searching.

After a while ashes and dust covered even the tips of the roofs. When people looked toward Pompeii, they saw only a hill. Those who were alive when Vesuvius exploded became old and died. No one remembered there had ever been a city called Pompeii.

The years went by. Vesuvius erupted again and again. More dust and ash piled on top of Pompeii and hardened.

Hundreds of years passed. The hill grew higher. When people climbed it, they never guessed a hidden city was buried under their feet.

Fifteen hundred years after the eruption that buried Pompeii, workmen dug up a riverbed. They dug so deep that their shovels struck part of an ancient building in Pompeii. They even found stones

A whole city—including piazzas and gardens—
had been buried for centuries. Those who found
Pompeii didn't even know it had been lost.

with the name "Pompeii" written on them. The name had been forgotten. No one imagined he had found a lost city. They didn't search any further.

In 1709 a man dug a deep well a few miles from where the stones had been found. As he scooped out the dirt, he uncovered part of the stage of a theater. It was from the old city of Herculaneum, which had been buried by Vesuvius at the same time Pompeii was. Workmen discovered vases, bronze statues, and pieces of marble.

Nobles living in the area liked the vases and statues the workmen had found. They began a treasure hunt to find as many as they could.

The nobles hired peasants and used hundreds of criminals to excavate, or dig out, the city. They dug tunnels and broke walls with picks and spades. They took marble coverings from the buildings and cut out pictures, called "frescoes," which were painted on the walls.

Digging for treasure in Herculaneum was hard work and moved slowly. In some places Herculaneum was covered with 60 feet (18.3 m) of ash. The ash hardened because of the dampness there. After a while fewer valuable things were found. Digging was moved from Herculaneum to a new place where country people had found vases.

The new place was the ancient city of Pompeii.

*Many paintings
and frescoes
have been salvaged
from the ruins,
but many more
were stolen by
earlier excavators.*

VI

MESSAGES ON THE WALL

In 1748 workmen in Pompeii dug up a skeleton. Silver and bronze coins lay beside it. It was the skeleton of a man who was killed by Vesuvius that fateful day in A.D. 79. He had been carrying the coins as he ran from the volcano—nearly 1,700 years earlier.

Workers did not yet know the name of the city where the skeleton was found. In 1763 they discovered that it was the lost city of Pompeii.

It was easier to dig at Pompeii than at Herculaneum. The city was buried under only 20 feet (6.1 m) of ash and pumice, rather than the 60 feet (18.3 m) of harder ash that covered Herculaneum. Within a few years, workmen dug out whole streets lined with rows of houses from ancient Pompeii.

Foreign rulers fought to control Italy. Often when a war broke out, workmen had to stop digging in Pompeii and become soldiers. For the next hundred years excavations started and stopped many times. Then, in 1860, foreign rulers were driven out of Italy, and Pompeii became part of a united Italy.

A short time later, the Italian archaeologist, Giuseppe Fiorelli, took charge of the excavations at Pompeii. Fiorelli put an end to the reckless treasure hunts. And he invented a way to show what the people of Pompeii looked like when they were killed by the volcano.

Over the years, the ash covering the bodies of people killed by Vesuvius had become hard. The bodies under the ash decayed and left spaces in the ash that were shaped like the people.

Fiorelli poured liquid plaster into the spaces. He let the plaster harden. Then he chipped off the ash all around the plaster casts that had been formed. This left plaster figures the exact size and shape of

Excavations were easier at Pompeii than at Herculaneum. Here, an archaeologist pieces a mosaic back together.

the people who died. They showed the expressions on people's faces and the shape of their clothing.

Fiorelli wanted to find out the names of the people of Pompeii. And he wanted to know who owned the buildings that were uncovered. In some houses he found rings with the owner's signature. Men of Pompeii had used them to seal letters. But he only found rings in a few homes.

Matteo Della Corte, who worked with Fiorelli, had an idea about how to find out the owners' names. When Vesuvius erupted, Pompeii was getting ready for elections. In those days, people painted signs or scrawled messages on their houses in their Latin language which told their own name and asked people to vote for their favorite candidate. If a sign said, "Vesonius Primus asks the voters to elect Gavius for office," Della Corte knew that Vesonius Primus owned the house. Della Corte identified over fifty homeowners by using election signs.

Sometimes the signs were jokes. One sign said the thieves wanted people to vote for a certain man. Another said the town drunks wanted them to vote for someone else.

Election notices were not the only wall writing, or graffiti. People of Pompeii might scratch a note about almost anything.

This plaster figure's position conveys the desperation the man felt in his final moments.

"May you sneeze sweetly," was the Roman way of saying "Good luck."

Schoolchildren scribbled complaints about punishment from mean teachers. "I was whipped for the third time," one child wrote.

An innkeeper bragged about the food he served. His note said, "Once one of my hams is cooked and set before the customer . . . he licks the pan in which it was cooked."

Advertisements and other wall writings told about gladiator contests at Pompeii's amphitheater, or stadium, which held 20,000 people. Sometimes gladiators fought each other. Sometimes they fought wild animals, such as lions or bears. Often the fights went on until someone was killed. Men dragged dead bodies from the arena with a large metal hook.

Advertisements like this were found on the walls of Pompeii: "Troop of 10 gladiators provided by D. Lucretius . . . will fight at Pompeii. . . . There will be a big hunt and awnings." The awnings were to protect the crowd from the blazing sun.

Two thousand years ago, winning gladiators were as popular as movie stars and rock stars are today. Someone scratched this note on the wall about a popular gladiator:

Celadus is the heartthrob of all the girls

Gladiators even scrawled notes about their victories. These were written on the walls of the gladiator barracks in Pompeii:

Severus—55 fights—has just won again

The unbeaten Hermiscus was here

Auctus of the Julian troop has won fifty times

No one knows if these gladiators escaped when Mt. Vesuvius exploded.

VII

THE LAST EIGHTEEN HOURS

The writing on the walls told about ordinary things in Pompeii. It showed daily life before the volcano changed everything. On that last day in Pompeii, people did not have time to scratch messages on the wall. The story of the fight against death is told by skeletons, plaster casts, and things people left behind.

Signs of hurry and panic have been found all over the city. Shops and other businesses were dug out hundreds of years after Vesuvius erupted, but the workmen who dug them out felt as though the owners had just fled a few minutes earlier.

The coins dropped by the shopkeeper still lay on the counter when the building was uncovered.

At a jewel worker's shop, precious stones were piled up, waiting for the jeweler to go on with his work. Many of the stones were already polished.

It was lunchtime when Vesuvius erupted, so many people in Pompeii were cooking their lunch or eating it. Normal life stopped before they could finish their meal, and the food stayed in its place for at least 1,700 years.

In one house, cooking pots were found with bones from meat that was put on to cook in August of A.D. 79. In another house, workers discovered the pig that was left roasting in the oven.

Workmen discovered the eggs and fish that the priests left on the table. Before they fled, the priests gathered statues and other temple treasures. They threw them into a cloth sack and ran, but they died trying to escape. The treasures were found near the place where the priests fell dead. Even as Vesuvius was exploding, one couple grabbed their gold, jewels, and silver dishes. They died with their treasures beside them.

Eighteen people hid in the cellar of a large house. All of them choked to death. A father lifted his arm to crawl to his children. He was killed, and his arm was frozen in the raised position. A mule driver choked as he sat pulling his blanket over his face. Plaster casts show what these terrified people looked like at the moment they died.

This plaster cast of a dog fighting to free himself is world famous.

Excavators found no sign of the gladiators who were relaxing in the wine shop. Their trumpets, used to announce the fights, were there. Perhaps those gladiators escaped.

At the gladiator barracks, many died. Skeletons of thirty-four gladiators were found in one room. Two more died in the barracks' jail. No one had stopped to free them.

And no one remembered to free the dog chained inside the house. A plaster cast shows the dog twisting as it tried to escape.

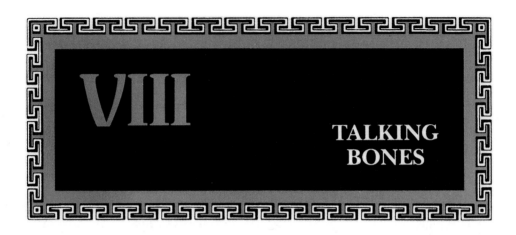

VIII

TALKING BONES

Many of the skeletons and spaces showing where people died in Pompeii were discovered a long time ago. In recent years, few skeletons have been found. Not long ago, though, whole families of skeletons were uncovered in another city buried by Vesuvius in A.D. 79.

In 1980 workmen were digging in the old city of Herculaneum, eight miles from Pompeii. As they dug, the men discovered an ancient skeleton. They kept digging and found three more skeletons.

Then, in 1982, workers explored shelters near the beach in Herculaneum, where ancient Romans kept their boats. They found dozens of skeletons. Scientists were amazed. Before this, they had found

*Most Herculaneum residents escaped before
their city was covered by the sixty feet
of hard ash that preserved it.*

few traces of dead people in Herculaneum. They had thought, therefore, that most Herculaneans had escaped. Now they knew that a large group of people had run to the beach, hoping to get away by boat. They were trapped there and killed by a river of gases and ash from Vesuvius.

Sara Bisel, an American expert in ancient bones, flew to Italy and began working on the skeletons. First, she washed the bones with a toothbrush and let them dry. Then she dipped them in a special liquid to make them stronger and keep them from crumbling. To Dr. Bisel, these bones are talking bones. They tell about ancient people.

The skeleton of a fourteen-year-old girl held a baby's skeleton in her arms. Dr. Bisel knew the baby was from a rich family, because she was wearing jewelry. Some people thought the fourteen-year-old was the baby's sister.

Dr. Bisel did not think so. The girl had a deep line on her teeth. It showed that at a young age she did not get enough to eat. On her arm bone was a scar caused by heavy work. Dr. Bisel knew a girl from a rich family would not have worked that hard. She decided the girl must have been a slave.

A skeleton of a Roman soldier with his sword and dagger was found on the beach. He was about thirty-seven years old, and was five feet eight and a half inches tall, slightly taller than the average Roman man. From the first skeletons Dr. Bisel studied in Herculaneum, she found that the average height of men was five feet seven inches (1.7 m).

The bones showed that the soldier's leg muscles were strong enough to ride bareback. That made sense because Romans did not use saddles. His right shoulder bone was rounded. This may have been caused by many years of throwing the javelin. Three missing front teeth were probably knocked out in a fight. And a spear wound could have made the lump Dr. Bisel found on his leg bone. This man was a strong soldier, who had survived wars and fights. He could not survive the nightmare of Vesuvius. He died on the beach, possibly trying to control the panicked crowd.

Dr. Bisel gave some of the skeletons special names. One lady wore gold earrings, heavy gold bracelets shaped like snakes, and two large gold rings. She was called "the ring lady."

Another skeleton was called "the helmsman" because he was found near a boat with an oar. He was in a different layer of ash than the others. Dr. Bisel thought he was drowned while out in his boat and then washed up on the beach.

The skeleton of a twenty-five-year-old pregnant lady, whose blond hair still stuck to her skull, was found. Among her bones, scientists found the skeleton of a seven-month-old unborn baby. It was still growing inside its mother when they were both killed. Dr. Bisel reported that putting the unborn baby's skeleton together was "like handling broken eggshells." The bones could break that easily.

Before the skeletons were discovered, many objects had been found in Herculaneum that told about life in the cities around Vesuvius.

One of the early discoveries was a whole library of books written on papyrus scrolls. Trying to unroll them was a problem. The scrolls were so old that as soon as the workmen's hands touched them the papyrus crumbled away. A priest invented a wooden frame to help keep the scrolls from crumbling.

In digging out one of the houses, something like an imprint of a cross was found. This suggested that Christians lived in the house. If it really is a cross, it may have been one of the first ones ever used as a sign of the Christian religion.

Of all the things found in Herculaneum, the skeletons have attracted the most attention. Altogether, over two hundred and fifty human skeletons and two skeletons of horses were discovered near the beach in the 1980s.

Although no skeletons have been found in Pompeii recently, some may still be hidden there. There are places inside and outside the walls of Pompeii that have not yet been excavated. People all over the world wonder what secrets are still buried there.

This beautiful patio was a secret for hundreds of years. There may still be beautiful areas to be discovered in Pompeii.

IX WILL THE NIGHTMARE RETURN?

In A.D. 79, Vesuvius buried Pompeii and turned it into a giant time capsule. Today, millions of people visit the city. They want to see what life was like in ancient times.

Visitors cram through the old sea gate. Crowds gather at the Forum. Tour guides speaking Spanish, German, Italian, English, and other languages lead people through the city. Groups of Italian schoolchildren on field trips join the crowds.

Not all parts of the city are crowded. People walk down some streets with only stray dogs for company. They look through remains of ancient shops that once sold hot and cold drinks, olive oil, bronze lamps, and other items.

Visitors pass the large grindstones once turned by slaves or animals to make flour for bread and even for dog biscuits. They visit the ancient baths.

They look through the gate of a house where a picture of a dog is part of the mosaic floor. The Latin words *Cave Canem* are written under the picture. This means "Beware of the dog."

People feel the horror of the last hours of Pompeii as they look at the plaster cast of the mule driver with his chin in his hands, or the family who suffocated in the garden.

Tourists walk to the large amphitheater. They stroll around the arena that was once covered with sand to soak up the blood of gladiators and wild animals. Today no vicious animals appear. Only a few lizards dart past.

Visitors sit in the seats of the empty amphitheater and look at Vesuvius in the distance. Today the mountain seems peaceful, just as it did in A.D. 79; but Vesuvius is not a peaceful mountain. It is an active volcano.

Scientists study the volcano constantly. They are on twenty-four-hour alert in case of changes. They cannot tame the volcano; they can only warn people if there are signs of danger.

The last eruption of Vesuvius was in 1944. It has erupted about fifty times since Pliny the Younger

Left: Just like residents did centuries ago, you can walk into this ancient shop that sold hot and cold food and drinks. Below: The amphitheater is a more peaceful place than it was before Vesuvius's fatal eruption.

Vesuvius stands over the excavated ruins.
Nothing could be done if the volcano should
erupt again like it did in A.D. *79.*

first watched it explode. Before each eruption, an earthquake has shaken the ground a year or more earlier. In 1980 an earthquake rocked Pompeii and other cities near the mountain. Scientists think another eruption is coming.

Vesuvius could once again cover Pompeii with ash and burning rocks.

When a city is at the foot of a volcano, safety cannot be guaranteed.

FOR FURTHER READING

Andrews, Ian. *Pompeii.* New York: Cambridge University Press, 1987.

Andrews, Ian. *Pompeii.* Minneapolis, Minnesota: Lerner Publications, 1980.

Goor, Ron, and Nancy Goor. *Pompeii: Exploring a Roman Ghost Town.* New York: Crowell Junior Books, 1986.

Hills, C. A. *The Destruction of Pompeii and Herculaneum.* North Pomfret, Vermont: David & Charles, Inc., 1987.

Kunhardt, Edith. *Pompeii . . . Buried Alive!* New York: Random House, 1987.

Rosen, Mike. *The Destruction of Pompeii.* New York: Bookwright Press, 1988.

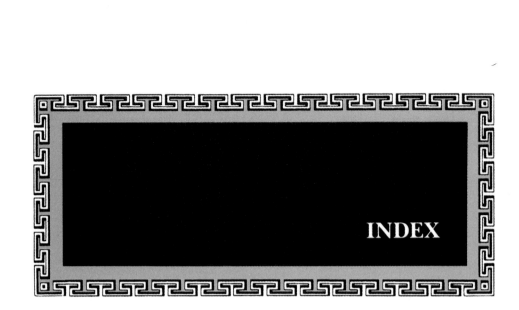

INDEX

ESCAPE FROM DEATH:
A Letter from Pliny the Younger to Tacitus

introduced and translated by Anne Ridley

Pliny the Younger wrote two letters about the eruption of Mount Vesuvius to the Roman historian Tacitus. They are the only eyewitness accounts of the disastrous eruption of Mount Vesuvius in A.D. 79. In the letter excerpt that follows, Pliny tells about what he personally did and observed during those dangerous three days.

Pliny the Younger also refers to his uncle, Pliny the Elder, in this letter. The elder Pliny was a Roman writer, scientist, and navy commander. He lived with his sister and nephew in Misenum, a town on the bay opposite the volcano.

When Mount Vesuvius began to erupt on an August day in A.D. 79 — for the first time in hundreds of years — Pliny the Elder decided to go by boat to observe the eruption, as well as to rescue some of the people trapped at the base of the mountain across the bay. Pliny the Younger turned down an invitation to go with him. As a result, he lived to write this account, which has been translated from the Latin.

This painting by French artist Pierre-Jacques Volaire depicts an eruption of Mount Vesuvius in 1779.

[65]

FROM PLINY'S LETTER

After my uncle left, I spent the rest of the day studying. Then I took my bath, ate dinner, and slept briefly and restlessly.

For many days, small earthquakes had been taking place, less terrifying because we were used to them in Campania. That night they became so strong that we easily believed that everything was not only shaking but, in fact, being turned upside down.

My mother came bursting into my room. I was just getting up, planning to wake her up if she was still asleep. We sat down in the area between our house and the sea. I do not know whether to call it courage or foolishness — I was seventeen — but I asked for a book to read. One of my uncle's friends, who had just returned from

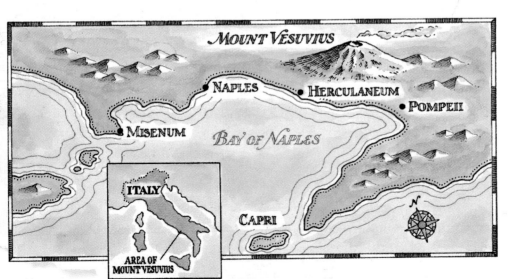

Pliny the Younger observed the eruption of Mount Vesuvius in A.D. 79 from Misenum. The map shows the area in the region of Campania affected by the eruption.

This painting by Swiss-born artist Angelica Kauffman in 1785 shows Pliny the Younger and his mother being warned of the danger from the erupting mountain.

Spain, came in. When he saw my mother and me sitting down and me reading a book, he scolded her for her lack of concern and me for my lack of fear. I kept on reading my book.

It was now about six in the morning, and the first light of day was weak and dim. The houses nearby were shaking. Although we were outside, the area was closed in and the fear of houses crashing down was great. At last it seemed best to leave town.

A frightened crowd followed, pushing and shoving those who were leaving as if they were in a huge marching line. We paused. We suffered many strange happenings, many fears. The carriages, which we had ordered to be brought out, were rolling in all directions, even though they were on level ground. They could not hold steady in the tracks. We saw the sea being swallowed into itself, as if being driven back by the tremor of the earth. The beach had moved out into the sea, revealing many of the sea's creatures on its dry sands.

From another direction a black and awful cloud, bursting with twisting and flashing streams of hot vapor, ripped open, revealing long, fiery flashes. They were similar to flashes of lightning, but larger.

Then my uncle's friend insisted, "If your brother is alive, he wants you to be safe. If he is dead, he would have wanted you to live. Why delay?" We answered that we could not think about our own safety until we were certain about his. Without delay, he departed from the danger in a burst of speed.

A little while later the cloud fell upon the land, covered the seas, and encircled the island of Capri, which then lay hidden. At that point my mother begged me, urged me, even ordered me to escape in whatever way I could. She said I was able to do so, being young, and that she, now old and heavy, would die well, knowing that she was not the cause of my death. I said that I would not be safe except with her along beside me. Then, grabbing onto her arm, I forced her to hurry onward. She obeyed me, painfully, and blamed herself for holding me back.

This painting by North American artist Ken Marschall shows what it may have been like in Herculaneum when Mount Vesuvius started to erupt.

Now came the ash, though it was still thin. I looked back: thick darkness was at our backs, running after us like a roaring stream rushing upon the earth. "Let's turn away while we can still see, so that we won't be crushed and trampled in the road by the crowd of people around us in the dark." We had barely sat down when darkness followed, not like the darkness of a cloudy night or a night without a moon, but like a closed room in which all light has been snuffed out.

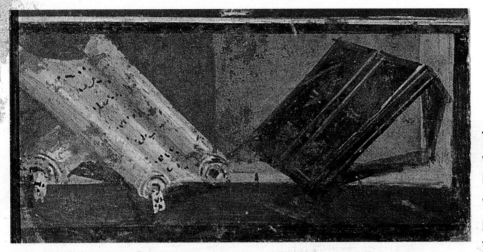

This fragment of a wall painting from Herculaneum shows writing materials used in the first century A.D. Shown from left to right are two papyrus book scrolls and a two-leafed wooden writing tablet.

You could hear the shrieking of women, the wailing of babies, the shouting of men. With their voices, some were seeking their parents, others their children, still others their husbands or wives. With their voices, they were trying to find each other.

Some were filled with sorrow over their own fate, others over the fate of their loved ones. There were those who, though afraid of death, were also praying for it to happen. Many lifted their hands to the gods, but more of them came to the conclusion that there were not gods anymore and that this was the final night for the world. There were also those who magnified the real dangers with lies and untruths. There were those who were quick to report to anyone who would believe them that now one part of Misenum had fallen, and now another part was on fire.

Then there was some brightening, but it was not like daylight. Instead, it was like the sign of an advancing fire. Then darkness returned and, with it, a lot of heavy ash. We stood up and began shaking it off, again and again. If we had not done this, we would have been crushed by its weight. I made myself feel better by believing that I was not dying alone, that everything else in the world was perishing with me.

Soon the real day returned and the sun came out. It was a pale yellow, as it is when in an eclipse. To our frightened eyes, everything seemed changed. Everything was covered with ash, as if it were a deep snow. Returning to Misenum, we spent an anxious night, not knowing whether to be fearful or hopeful. Fear held us as the earthquake continued. Several people, driven crazy, joked about their fate and everyone else's fate by crying out terrible predictions. My mother and I were not planning to leave until we received word about my uncle, however, even though we had already experienced danger and were expecting still more of it.

Read what I have written, but do not write it down because it is not good enough for your history book. You are to blame, since you are the one who asked for it, if you do not even think my recollections good enough for a letter. Farewell.

Double inkwells such as this one held black and red inks for writing. The usual writing tools were sharpened quill or reed pens. Less often, pens were made of copper or bronze.

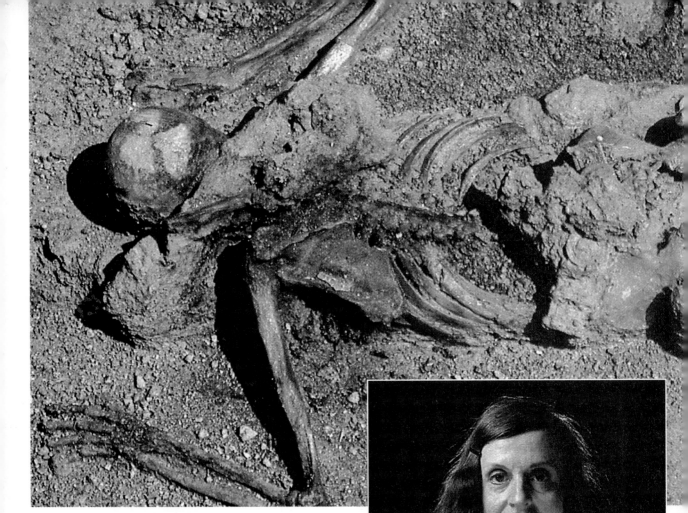

SARA BISEL

THE BONE LADY

by Shannon Brownlee

Top: At the ancient Roman resort of Herculaneum, this skeleton of a soldier sprawls face-down in the mud, his sword still at his side, a knapsack containing carpenter's tools still slung across his back. Inset: Sara Bisel and one of her subjects pose for a portrait.

Herculaneum has changed little in 2,000 years. Mounds of beans and corn and a silver ring still sit just where the greengrocer Aulus Fufer left them. Down the street, a delicate, half finished cameo and an uncut aquamarine rest on a jeweler's workbench, ready for a practiced hand to take them up once again. In the House of Telephus a modest lunch lies half eaten — rolls, cakes, eggs still in their shells.

On August 24, A.D. 79, a deafening blast from Mount Vesuvius shot a column of smoke and debris twelve miles into the stratosphere, burying both Herculaneum, a beautiful Roman seaside resort, and nearby Pompeii. Eighteen centuries later, an excavator found in Pompeii hollow casts made of the ash that had suffocated thousands of Pompeiians and then solidified around them; their bodies decomposed, leaving the hollow molds. No such remains were discovered at Herculaneum, which led historians to believe its inhabitants had escaped.

However, in 1982 workers digging a trench near what was once the city's port on the Bay of Naples happened on a

Mount Vesuvius

Pompeii

Naples

Herculaneum

Bay of Naples

macabre find: the skeletons of dozens of Herculaneans, struck down as they huddled inside stone chambers used to store boats. About seven hours before the Pompeiians smothered in ash, a frothy avalanche of gases, pumice, and rock hurtled down the mountainside toward Herculaneum. Traveling at over 80 miles an hour, it blasted through ceilings, windows, and doors to suffocate the Herculaneans. Later waves entombed the city and preserved their bones in an airtight casing of rock.

One hundred yards from the boat sheds and their grisly contents, Sara Clark Bisel sits in a cavernous one-room laboratory at the Herculaneum museum, holding the clean and shining thighbone of a Herculanean. More than a hundred yellow plastic crates, the kind ordinarily used to hold vegetables in Italian markets, line the shelves of her laboratory, each containing a skeleton lifted from the mud. Bisel, known in archaeological circles as

The Neapolitan coastline of Italy sits at the foot of a dangerous neighbor: Mount Vesuvius, which exploded in A.D. 79, raining a lethal shower of ash on Pompeii that suffocated its residents. Nearby Herculaneans were buried under a glowing avalanche of volcanic debris that cooled to form a 60-foot layer of light rock, called tuff.

the Bone Lady, is in charge of preserving the skeletons at Herculaneum. "Bones are nice to feel," she says, gently stroking the ancient thighbone. "They like to be fussed over, and they tell me their histories."

The more superstitious Neapolitans think *la dottoressa Sara* is a bit dotty to spend so much time with bones, but her job is to glean all the information she can from the skeletons — which constitute one of the most significant archaeological finds of the century. Ancient Romans usually cremated their dead, leaving few direct clues to their physical characteristics. The few hundred skeletons at Herculaneum offer a wealth of new information.

Bisel is a physical anthropologist, which requires her to act simultaneously as forensics expert, chemist, and artist. She specializes in reconstructing and measuring shattered skulls and skeletons in order to recover the lost histories of the ancient peoples of the Mediterranean. Like a growing number of her colleagues, she takes advantage of developments in chemistry and forensics to deduce the health and diets of her subjects.

Bisel, who is now in her early fifties, was a housewife in Rochester, Minnesota, only thirteen years ago. Despite her relative newness to the field of anthropology, her credentials include studies in nutrition, art, chemistry, and archaeology, as well as anthropology. She began work at Herculaneum in 1982, on the recommendation of J. Lawrence Angel of the Smithsonian Institution, a leading expert on the Mediterraneans of antiquity. Looking for help, Italian authorities had consulted Angel, who considered Bisel perfect for the Herculanean task. Out of hundreds of physical anthropologists, he says, "I can think of only two other people as suitable."

Five acres of Herculaneum lie exposed in a huge pit in the dismal modern city of Ercolano, a suburb of Naples. Four miles distant, the profile of the still dangerous Vesuvius looms. Against this backdrop, clad in jeans and a tank top, Bisel stoops to gather her latest batch of bones. Inside her

Right: At the excavation site in Herculaneum, the boat sheds contained many skeletons.

Below: In one of the recently unearthed boat sheds of Herculaneum, several dozen skeletons lie huddled as if they were sheltering each other.

With deft fingers and an eye for the human form, Bisel reconstructs a broken skull.

laboratory, the skeletons of 48 men, 38 women, and 25 children have made their way into the yellow plastic boxes, but only after a lengthy process.

After washing each bone, she dips it in an acrylic solution to preserve it and sets it on a rack to dry. Many of the bones, particularly the skulls, are broken. With an artist's eye for the human form, Bisel often spends two days painstakingly reassembling

the fragments with glue and linking missing sections with wire. Then she measures the skull, pelvis, vertebrae, and twelve long bones of the skeleton.

From her observations and measurements, Bisel has constructed vivid accounts of Roman life. She pulls down a crate and holds up the skull of a man nicknamed the Soldier. "He's so macho," says Bisel. "He was muscular, and 68 inches tall — one of the tallest men so far. They were small people compared to us." Men were on the average only 67 inches tall, and women only 61 inches. Pointing to a ridge in an arm bone called the deltoid crest, Bisel says, "From his sword and belt we know he was a soldier. From his deltoid crest, I know he was a manual laborer. You can see the bone has been remodeled to accommodate a large muscle."

Bisel turns to another crate, rummaging for a pelvic bone. "This is the second pregnant woman I've seen here, and she was just a kid herself — only sixteen years old." Bisel holds out a bone, translucent and fragile as a bird's. "The fetus was seven and a half months old. The girl's pelvis is so small, she might have died in childbirth if she hadn't been caught by Vesuvius. Better to die quickly from asphyxiation than after three days of labor."

One by one Bisel tells their tales. Each cleaned and measured skeleton reveals its owner's age, sex, size; taken together, they form a mosaic of life styles, diets, and diseases. "The connection between health and civilization is often overlooked," she says. "Skeletons give the best clues to the health of a population." Running her fingernail along a leg bone, she explains that a rough patch was almost certainly caused by a blood-borne infection — most likely staphylococcus. "People now don't remember what it was like before penicillin," she remarks. "In those days if you got an infection it could hang on for years."

Some skeletons show evidence of anemia, arthritis, or abscesses, but in general the Romans that Bisel has examined were robust, muscular, healthy people. To discover what they ate, Bisel ground up bone from the tibia and analyzed its mineral content. The condition of the bones and the minerals they contained told Bisel the Romans had a balanced diet. The level of strontium, a mineral found in plants and the flesh of fish, indicated that they ate more fish than animal protein. Bisel found one group that was not so healthy: slaves. The teeth of a 14-year-old girl revealed malnutrition, and the bones of her arms and shoulders showed the marks of heavy labor. "I find it sad that little kids had to work that hard," she says.

Above: In her Torre del Greco hotel room, Bisel relaxes with an Italian newspaper.

Above: A Roman house key.

"These skeletons were found with keys in their hands. I find that very touching. They all thought they would be going home again."

TREASURES FROM THE ASHES

Glass drinking cup This drinking cup was made of cobalt blue glass. The body of the cup was formed by blowing it into a mold. Stemmed goblets like these were used at banquets.

The volcanic eruption that buried Pompeii and Herculaneum in A.D. 79 also preserved many of their artifacts. These treasures give us fascinating glimpses of the lives and times of the people who lived there.

Glass jugs Here are two small glass jugs used to hold liquids. Hand-blown by a glassblower, these jugs were made in different shapes and colors.

Panel with theater masks The masks worn by stage actors made popular home decorations too. This marble relief panel, in which the carving stands out from a flat background, probably was set on a low column in a garden. This side of the panel shows three deeply carved comic masks with a temple front at the upper left.

Pottery Clay containers such as these were used for storing and transporting liquids and different kinds of foods.

Mosaics Mosaic pictures made of small colored pieces of stone or glass decorated the walls and floors of many homes in Pompeii. This mosaic shows a group of actors rehearsing for a play. Face masks worn on stage are shown at the feet of the seated figure and to his right. The actual size of the mosaic pieces is shown to the right of the mosaic.

Bronze kettle This bronze kettle was found at Pompeii. Highly detailed, the pot has a pointed lid and sits on three elaborate lion's paws.

Gold bulla A *bulla* was a small, bag-shaped charm that was worn around the neck. Sons of Roman citizens wore the gold bulla to show their birthright until they grew to manhood.

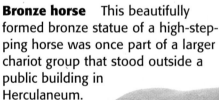

Bench This finely made bronze bench was called in Latin a *bisellium* or "seat of double width." Cushions placed on it made it comfortable for sitting.

Bronze horse This beautifully formed bronze statue of a high-stepping horse was once part of a larger chariot group that stood outside a public building in Herculaneum.

Oil lamp Standing oil lamps such as this provided lighting at night. This bronze lamp had a single nozzle for a wick. Some lamps had up to fourteen nozzles, which increased the amount of light and smoke they gave off.